Behind The Phonics

The idea behind our colorful picture book was inspired by Pamela Marfisi, who through years of teaching found these techniques to be the most successful tools in teaching young children the fundamentals of phonics, during the early reading development stages.

It is our great pleasure to open up the fun world of phonics, through the engaging story of Miss Cow Goes To Town.

ISBN: 978-0692047118

East Atlantic Publications

The artwork of this book was hand illustrated before digitally designed.

The text is set in Comic Sans MS.

Edited By Pamela Marfisi.

Idea By Pamela Marfisi.

Designed by Anna Marfisi.

Marfisi, Anna, 2017 - author, illustrator.

Miss Cow Goes To Town / written and illustrated by Anna Marfisi.

Miss Cow Goes To Town

Written and Illustrated by

Anna Marfisi

Miss Cow went to town in a brown gown.

Miss Cow found a crown on the ground.

"W<u>ow</u>!" sh<u>ou</u>ted Miss C<u>ow</u>

a br<u>ow</u>n cr<u>ow</u>n.

Mouse House

Bow Wow Shop

Hound Pound

Ground Coffee

Lost and Found

Brown Shop

Town Gowns

Cloud Downs

Sow's Flower Shop

Miss Cow bounded for town with her brown gown and her newfound crown.

"Miss Cow!" howled Sir Hound and shouted Miss Sow.

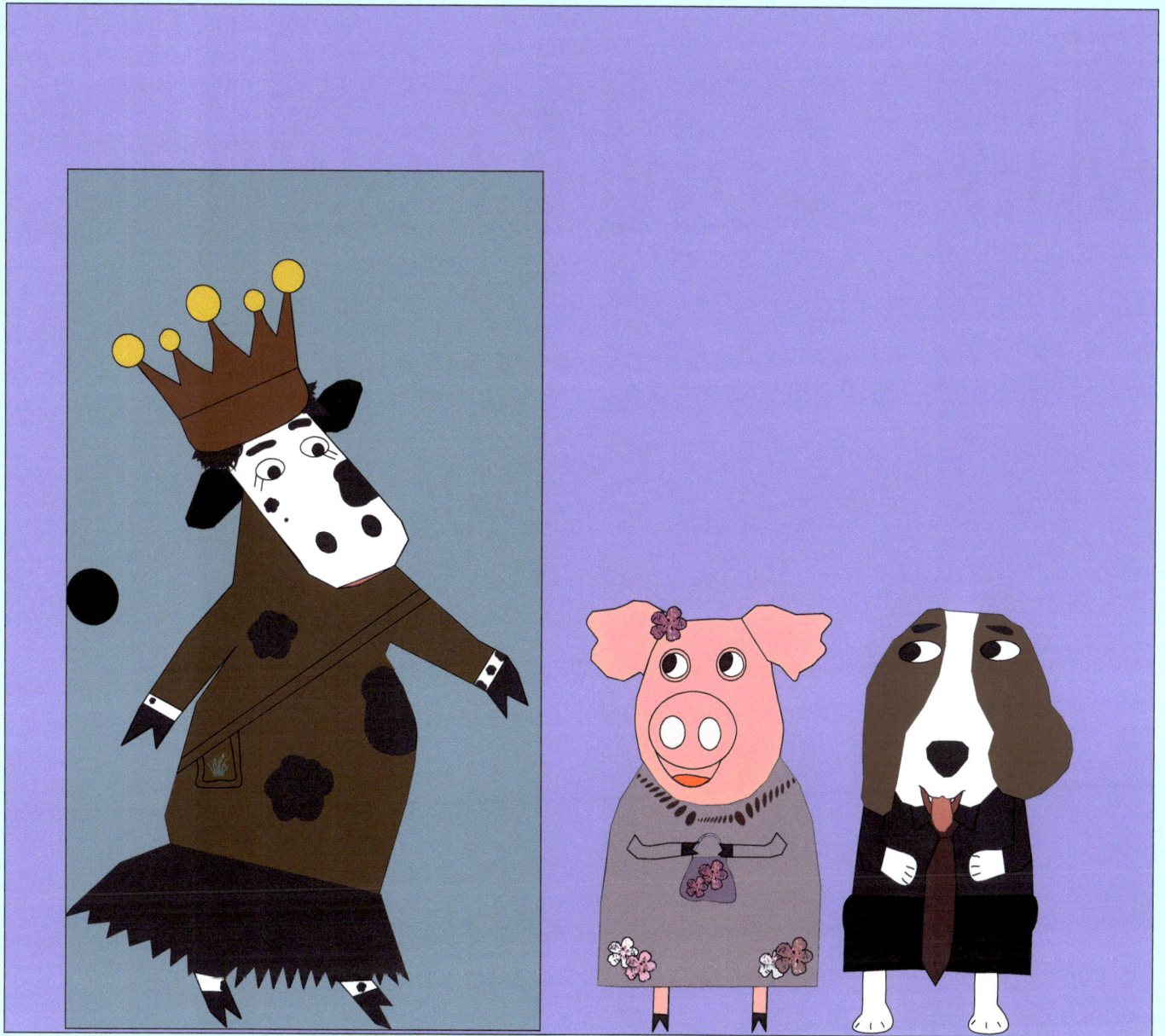

Sir H<u>ou</u>nd and Miss S<u>ow</u> wore br<u>ow</u>n, but not a cr<u>ow</u>n like Miss C<u>ow</u>.

Miss C<u>ow</u> Fr<u>ow</u>ned.

Not a s<u>ou</u>nd Sir H<u>ou</u>nd or Miss S<u>o</u>w said that made Miss C<u>ow</u>'s fr<u>ow</u>n turn from d<u>ow</u>n.

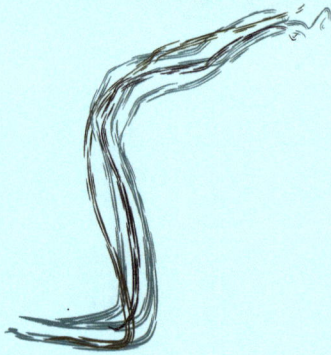

Miss Cow found a mound of brown ground away from town.

Miss Cow pouted on her brown mound, but no one was about to see her pout.

Miss Cow's crown beside her brown gown.

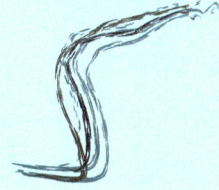

Down from town was
Miss Cow's grounds.

Where Sir Hound and Miss Sow found mounds to sit down.

"D<u>ow</u>n," Miss C<u>ow</u> p<u>ou</u>ted, not a h<u>ou</u>nd, nor a s<u>ow</u>, to turn her fr<u>ow</u>n.

"Miss C**ow**?" announced a m**ou**se in his h**ou**se.

On the gr<u>ou</u>nd where the cr<u>ow</u>n was f<u>ou</u>nd was Sir M<u>ou</u>se that lived in a cr<u>ow</u>n.

Sir Mouse wore a crown brown as Miss Cow's crown.

Miss Cow's frown was turned upside down, proud she bounded for town with her crown.

Sir Mouse bounded for town in a crowned house atop a cow.

"Miss Cow!" shouted Sir Hound and Miss Sow with brown crowns they found on the ground.

Miss C<u>ow</u>, Sir H<u>ou</u>nd, and Miss S<u>ow</u> bounced from t<u>ow</u>n to Miss C<u>ow</u>'s gr<u>ou</u>nds.

Sir H<u>ou</u>nd pr<u>ou</u>d of his newf<u>ou</u>nd cr<u>ow</u>n.

While Miss Cow found her brown crown no longer turned her frown from down.

But the mouse in his house,
that found a vow to never
frown.

While Sir Mouse found
a sow, a hound, and a cow,
as friends forever now.

In a h<u>ou</u>se fit
for a m<u>ou</u>se.